# On the Porch, Under the Eave

~

Jane Simpson

FUTURECYCLE PRESS
*www.futurecycle.org*

Copyright © 2017 Jane Simpson
All Rights Reserved

Published by FutureCycle Press
Athens, Georgia, USA

ISBN 978-1-942371-41-0

*for Amelia*

# Contents

What I Think About When I Peel Ginger Root .................... 7
Come Friday .................... 8
Slog and Stupor .................... 9
Behind the Eyelids .................... 10
Under the Honeysuckle Bower .................... 11
When Now We Gather .................... 12
When We Made Ice Cream .................... 13
The Family Legacy .................... 14
Summer Camp on Black Mountain .................... 15
Taking Driving Lessons from a Blind Man .................... 16
Ignorance Matters .................... 17
On Seeing Blake at the Tate, 1974 .................... 18
Turning 21 .................... 19
Permanent Wave .................... 20
I'm Not Sure If It Lessens the Import .................... 21
Panola Mountain .................... 22
This Is Not Another Poem About Dying .................... 23
Congressman Lewis Spoke About President Obama .................... 24
The Horticultural Therapist Works
    With a Patient in a Nursing Home .................... 26
When to Say Goodbye and Thanks .................... 27
She Would've Hated What I Chose .................... 28
I Try to Remember Before Her Dementia .................... 29
The Leisure of Belief to Regulate .................... 30
Washing Raspberries .................... 31
The Stain Looms .................... 32
Church Bells at Midnight .................... 33
I Live Only on Streets Named for Trees .................... 34
Acknowledgments

## What I Think About When I Peel Ginger Root

Someone once unearthed and dried yucca
to discover tapioca pearls.
How many ages did that take? How many
rib-sore souls folded when they stirred
the same root into cyanide?

Who first found the leaves of oleander
couldn't be steeped in a tea? That this greenery
wrung hearts and bowels, crumbled the hungry
into a forest corner where they saw light snake
with vines as they writhed on the ground.

Mushroom martyrs were felled by botany's
poison and their thirst was a fire. Water
was a fuel. The nausea, stench of emissions—
how many bodies failed to purge
and pardon to survive and eat again?

In doubt, did they test the unknown on the old,
the lame, the youngest orphans? Did they feed
the matted curs, leave tastes for field-mice?
Did they mark the first time they peeled and ate
the paper skin of a fire-roasted yam?

The starved couldn't weigh pangs with pains,
risked being planted with roots, herbs and shrubs.
Perhaps they gnawed shoots and savored the belch.
Maybe all were sated by the risk in the new
if the ginger root couldn't ease their cramps.

## Come Friday

On Friday I will coil like a cat
on the arm of a chair and look
into the sun. Then I will rise,
stretch, turn clockwise to study
how light walks across a room.

This day I will stop and press
my body into the hardwoods,
feel seams in the floorboards,
size up and seize how my breath
fits into the frame of my space.

It's then I will hum like a mud
dauber, craft fine Doric
columns and layer red-clay
textures around the adobe
on the porch under the eave.

Come Friday, I will talk and chew
at the same time, taste words letter
by letter, by vowel, by drawl.
Tongue the bitter and the guava,
swallow only that Peruvian moon.

## Slog and Stupor

What road today?
The steps of stupor
from the bed to the bath
are sure, but beyond?
To the sea by way
of the street to the sea?
Past the arch-spined
news vendor, the terrain
of the world clefting his face.
Past the child with a tincture
of earth around the toes,
the ankles, a foot clutching
the thong in a yellow flip-flop.
Past the produce stand—
melons baking in the fruited heat
of a sun not seen, obscured
by canopy, brows of shoppers
scrounging for the worm,
the worm that drops through
poke holes in sidewalk stands,
creeps, slither by slither,
down the street to the sea.
What road today?
Before the slog from bath to bed,
before the lids enclose
on the dark of the sea?

## Behind the Eyelids

I finger the bones
of *I am, I am not*
in a room cloaked
in blackout drapes.
A day stilled in night.

In the trip the earth
takes around the back-
yard of the sun,
I hear before I see
the drip of the rag-tied
water spigot.

I feel before I notice
the noise of the furnace.
I smell before I taste
yesterday's
onion in olive oil.

It's then I touch
the tender of the bruise,
note how the purples
flesh into an unlimited
sweep of the heavens.

## Under the Honeysuckle Bower

We were shade's children
playing in green weeds,
honeysuckle branches,
tatting a lace of reverence.
A sanctuary thicket
from the house and heat.

We were the children
of the harvest,
gathering our crop,
feeding from porcelain
cups the pearled
heart of plenty.

We were the children
at the fair
threading with skill
thin vines into garlands,
the surfeit incense
in the apse of simplicity.

We were the children
of grace
reveling in our bounty.
We didn't know that our
cloister would never
again be so full, so fragrant.

## When Now We Gather

Always, we tell of the outing to the country, to picnic
by a spring down a dirt road, how we gathered
grandparents, cousins, infants, scores
of us, and we hiked in Six Mile, South Carolina,
where my father led us past brambles, around ruts
on a search for the water—he was the dad who helped
his children, showed his small boy how to make an axe
from a wedge of wood and a two-by-four.
We packed overcooked fried chicken—the women
feared the shame of pink in a breast bone—toted pie tins
of devilled eggs, jars of sweet pickles, bottles of Coke.
The son with the axe, ever a busy boy, chopped ankles,
rotten logs, a turtle shell, a bee hive in a tree stump.
The hive was a clock at the moment of alarm.
A swarm teemed up, spread into fine, quick atoms
of surprise, diving onto babies, the old,
up the poodle skirt of my mother who stripped
without the pause of modesty to her slip,
onto all but the little boy with a toy axe.
We were covered with berried skin, plastered with wads
of Camel tobacco the men tore from their cigarettes.
We never made it to the spring, and if we had,
we would have little to share when now we gather
to bury our people who went looking for clear waters.

## When We Made Ice Cream

They'd call the smaller child least likely
to wriggle, so that'd be me, seat me
on the ice-cold and wet bar of the handle—
a narrow metal horse that froze my tiny ass.
They needed me to weight the bucket upright
when thick richness slowed the dasher
to the drag of cement-truck rotations.
I hated the way the water would soak
my shorts, my panties, ride up my shirt.
I hated the spill of the rock salt down
my legs, into the loose elastic
of my tube socks, into my red Keds.
I hated how my father would jostle
me with the twist of the crank, then growl,
*Hold still, keep your feet flat on the ground.*
But then the frozen moment, when no arm
could turn the clotted mass, when it took
gloved hands to twist the threads of the top,
pry it open and give me the paddle
to curl my tongue around that dull blade.
This is not about patience and merit,
yearning for dimly lit nights of childhood.
It's that I took my mother's boiled custard,
the high speed of the Sunbeam mixer,
a silver canister speckled with age.
It's that once my mouth sent to my brain
a hope, and I took the good, made
it a lament, antiquated and gone.

## The Family Legacy

Emily Dickinson would have baked
this cake when she sent gifts to offer
neighbors the solace of food. Her words
were tied in ribbons in the bedroom.

The recipe comes dog-eared and greasy,
the words of women who made homes and cakes,
only the butter and eggs tempered
to fill mouths, block verbs that choke stories.

This cake serves as a peace offering for rage,
a trough for sweetness. It's batter to fill
the veins of women drained of blood
they let for their children and husbands.

The women who make this cake cream butter
and sugar so light it's the softness they
touch—they use the tip of a little finger
to scoop a meager feeling onto the tongue.

The bakers beat their strain into eggs, pour
ease onto edges of bad days, then fold
in flour with a purpose that never
spills beyond their wilted aprons.

The women have an instinct for timing,
know the moment batter browns to crust.
Then, when the cake is done, they
lift up comfort and slice it into grandeur.

## Summer Camp on Black Mountain

The girl in the next cabin knew how to make
red high-tops, shorts look like an impulse,
how to stomp, with both feet, mushrooms
on a trail so they exploded into stem bombs,
how to trot in a ring at the closing program.
She showed skill of lifted wrist, straight back
and still her mother screamed—her horse
reared, rested tail and rump on the girl's spleen
which ripped and bled like crepe paper.
A girl and her horse—both named Bonnie—
were put down after a night when counselors
roused campers from their bunks at two a.m.,
herded them past the silhouette of mountain
laurel, in gowns, to bow uncombed heads
in the chapel. A hundred pious girls
knelt in the dream and drama of one plea.
That's the night I shivered on a stone floor
in the mountains of North Carolina,
heard the hoot and howl of the owl that perched
in the dark wood. I began then to stuff
words, prayers, chants down my throat to gag
the appeals because I'd known the screeches—
the avian-like moans that sounded
loudest in woods on a chill summer night.
I'd known the call, the beg, of a mother
who watched her child go cold.

## Taking Driving Lessons from a Blind Man

My father's glaucoma left him shuttered and silent
when he was in his forties, a man of a dark time:
no books, no ballgames, only flight from himself.
On Sunday afternoons, after dinner, his nap,
he would say to me, a sixteen-year-old, *Let's drive.*
I worried that tonnage wrapped in metal and speed
was an unguided risk, path to precipice and calamity,
yet we took to the roads—him brooding, leaning,
me clutching the wheel, engine, dread.
I'd round a curve, singe the tire on a curb. He'd say,
*Center it in the lane, look at the car ahead.*
Today I parallel park with skill, apply his math—
align mid-space to bisect an angle, pull up.
Success in economy. Practical methods for tight spots.
Our routes merged. I learned to drive.
He rode with his back to me and faced nothing.

## Ignorance Matters

House Speaker Tom Murphy would vote
for a cur over a Republican. He wasn't fair
or bipartisan. He didn't light up a room,
though his cigars stayed when he stormed out.
I learned even more when Channel 2 sent me
to intern at the Capitol where politicians
ambled, stiff knights dubbed blade on blade.
I sat that first day of the session, watched
from a window in the press box, saw
when the speaker took the podium, banged
a gavel and brought up a preacher from Cairo
to open the State with the Church. I saw him
sidle from the chamber. And when a doorkeeper
beckoned, said the Speaker wanted me
in his office, I followed. Murphy was waiting,
chair tilted, one leg crossed, ankle on knee.

He sat with his sides exposed as if he had guns
on his belt, and he asked my name, repeated it—
slow, polite. Then he began to yell,
he *went on,* said he would banish me
since I didn't stand for the prayer.
He questioned my upbringing, jammed his
cigar like a rifle butt on *rudeness* and *arrogance*.
I wasn't allowed a defense
and my tears made his tirade last longer.
This was the day I woke up and offended God,
the State, the Speaker of the House.
The day I brought shame on my employer,
family, school. Before lunch, before twenty.
But nothing happened. It didn't matter
that I sat, held in my lap accidental
power. That I blued temple veins.

## On Seeing Blake at the Tate, 1974

I'd go down to go up
in that corner,
that room where ink
smudged scritches of mercy,
scratches of pity.
I'd go there once, twice
a week, for weeks.
I'd sit, drawn
like smoke to smolder—
too young to know
why I went, old enough
to know there was mystery.
I'd stare at acid in etches
of the divine images
but I was schooled
in human form,
couldn't see the strokes
that marked
how mystery was to see.
Even now I return
when breaths taste
of diesel fuel, when air
enters as a gasp,
leaves as a sigh, when
to exhale is to expunge
and oxygen
purges and purifies.

## Turning 21

We were the girls who mocked the girls
who wore add-a-bead necklaces that draped
silk sternums dabbed in White Linen.
They were debs with dads who knew
at their births they would need two white
dresses—cotillion and wedding.
We did not want to be them, we wanted
to swoop, strike, exceed them.

Still, we baked, swept corner cobwebs
from Claire's daddy's farm in Anniston,
hauled burgers, buns, kegs. We wore long,
poly-washable dresses that rode cowboy
boots, topped with hats, bandanas,
or both. We added the allure of twenty-one.
We had a hundred people to our party—
boys from town, boys we wanted in town.

At dark Claire's beau hitched his jeep
to a hay wagon and we drove the sullen
back roads of Alabama.
When we saw the sheriff's car tailing
without lights, we hid the beer under hay.
Calhoun County was dry so we sang,
loud enough to merge field mice and owls—
*Jesus Loves Me,* which did not save us
since our driver didn't cut his hair or shave.
Claire's father rescued—Norman Rockwell
pipe at mouth to cover the Budweiser
smell, he said later—and the officer noted
a bad taillight, sent us into the night.

We went forth 'til our boys needed to pee.
They lined the side of the road in military order
and, at the count of three, streamed in unison.
We were the girls who squealed in the wagon,
covered our faces with our hands,
and hid from a night air of pee and pine needles.

## Permanent Wave

My hair nests in the trenches of the boar
bristles, soft finery that when pulled attaches
to my fingers and cannot be shaken off, like my
Southern mother who put a hard *g* on *darling,*
who baked the heat-and-serve rolls
until they had the shell of a walnut.
She would drive fifteen miles to the only beauty
parlor in the county—Dot's—who still lubed,
coiled wiry strands on pink rods and set them
under a hood to dry, her shop in a garage
behind the house with pictures of red-lipped
beauties taped to a pine-paneled wall.
My mother's curls had meaning—glamour,
grace, since no cherub on the soap dish
ever had straight hair.
She and her mother-in-law, who knew
how to give home perms, once annointed
my brain with ammonia so strong it reeked
past the stop sign on the corner, jumped
the tracks and rode the train out of Decatur.
Come Monday morning Mrs. Crudup
of the fourth grade would look up from roll
call and ask if I put my finger in a socket.
My mother's words when my husband
downed six bottles of pills with a rum chaser:
*Maybe you should get a perm.*
She wanted so much more for me—short
ringlets sprayed hard against the scalp—
a kind of Valkyrie's helmet. Or it might
look like a flourish of baby's breath to soften
the look I trained on her. Or maybe
I could grow controlled curls that would spring
from my padlock of a head, for her hasp and hold.

## I'm Not Sure If It Lessens the Import

to live so many defined moments
in dim-lit outdoor cafes, on May nights,
when the temperature is not either/or,
just *is,* and a mild breeze carries the moment.
One time three of us—me, our girl, her father—
sat in such a place, to celebrate;
but my daughter's commencement
really began years earlier
when we were family and then not.
I regret how the three of us splintered,
moved forward in hooded black raincoats,
heads hunched against the cold drizzle.
But that May night, in the star-strands of white
tree lights, we had no history,
and though we had no collective future,
we relished entrées broiled in the flavor
of the familiar and the familial.
There was the swap of words that didn't
pose or proffer, words that found roots, caves,
that became spore growing wild.
I heard in the father-daughter exchange
the swab of verbal DNA when he asked,
*What is that purple vine, it starts with an h?*
And she replied, *Oh, it's wisteria.*
And he said, *That's right—hysteria.*
I noted the Merlot-colored bloodlines
in the banter, the ease that came
with the absence of effort, and for once
we didn't need to read each other's faces
or utterances, and our heads glanced
down only to find the food on our plates.

## Panola Mountain

The November road
we're driving's
just another county
coroner's office—
'possums, deer, raccoons.
Even the yards seem
like they're something
else—they're peopled
in campaign signs.
The way to Panola Mountain's
narrow—eight churches,
seven miles, all the meat
and threes closed on this day.
You and I are here
to hike, go forward
in a future I can't see.
I'm sure I feel vagrant
spirits rise around us—
some old dead bodies—
and I really think they're
trooping stiff-legged uphill,
but nothing's as it seems.
Except you—still aloof,
so far ahead you merge
with trees and hanging vines.
I notice how the trail acorns
sink deeper into the earth
from your long-gone foot.

## This Is Not Another Poem About Dying

I thought the woman on the bed
in the next ICU room was resting—
without covers, pillows, tubes, monitors,
just a nap, arms at sides,
the way tanners strain to look relaxed,
face-up on the shore, slightly
angled to let the underarms breathe,
legs modestly veed so the crotch
senses the tease of air.
Her heels were pasty, finely cracked—
the insides of flea-market teacups.
She needed a blanket, I worried
when I drifted by on Monday.
It's about not knowing the dead.
On Tuesday, I learned she got a spade.
Someone had to shovel and lift dirt,
gently shake tendrils and roots.
I hoped they placed her close to the top
so she'd feel the pull of the sun.

## Congressman Lewis Spoke About President Obama

I lingered in the back of the nursing
home the day John Lewis visited,
saw him bend to shake hands that shook—
old veterans on the Fourth of July.
I'd forgotten he was an archer
whose shot arced straight to the heart
with what he said, the way he said it.
I heard his calm—that of a man who'd
learned the worst thing about being
alive was the people you lived among.

Lewis placed his hands at his sternum,
the tenor ready for the aria.
He spoke with a voice that entered body
space, with words that slipped
around the gray wisps that fringed
long lobes, and he began with how he'd
just come from Charleston,
how he'd gone
with President Obama
to eulogize Reverend Pinckney.

We all moved in to hear his story—
doubled-over, de-limbed vets
stretched their necks,
aides moved between walker handles,
I shifted to my toes.
Lewis explained how the people
in Carolina had sat that day
in funeral finery, listened
for memorial meaning—
he knew there was nothing

the President could say.
But in the nursing home that day
Lewis knitted a blessing

with a yarn spun in the fibers
of sinew and blood,
of spleen and gristle.
*Words alone don't comfort.*
              *So Obama preached,*
Lewis said. He told the old soldiers
how the president opened his mouth,

how he closed his mouth—
how for ten seconds he stood—
until he looked up and out, raised
his voice up and out, and sang
*Amazing Grace, how sweet the sound.*
In the coughs and tissue-lint of that room,
Lewis gave us sermon, song, silence—
gave it to all the grave people who need
what words can't say, when mouths can't
speak, on bad days when we want to listen.

# The Horticultural Therapist Works With a Patient in a Nursing Home

He unfolds the curls of her fingers—they look
like clear and yellow onions.
Before her muscles retract, he places a small plant.
He has handed a fly rod to a woman in a river
of glare and fish that leap like ocular migraines.

It's a cutting—a stick of stringy stalk, rotted fibers
of brown roots—nothing with promise, but the woman
leans in to her palms—her chin touches her chest—
she sees the potatoes in her father's garden, how she
would take her hands, mound the earth to cover the base.

She would sit on her haunches, knees in soft dirt, heels
under the hem of her dress. She'd dig into soil
with bare fingers and wear a cuticle ring of grit for days.

It wasn't a matter of scrubbing—dirt bled into her skin.
Her father gave her hilling as a chore—she didn't quit
until the potatoes were vaults in pyramids.
Her potatoes never scorched on the vine, nor did their
meat turn green. They were the bowl of steam and starch
on the dinner table, ochre streams of butter that ran
over lumps, into troughs, cracks in crockery.

The young man in blue scrubs cups her hands in his,
gives meaning to motion, gives life to what
the head but not the hand can hold—
the smell of earth after rain, thoughts that roll
in the scent of grass while the lawn mower cools.

## When to Say Goodbye and Thanks

When she reaches with a hurried hand
for the door, looking over her shoulder
the way she does, not at anyone, anything.
When her landscape is lit by headlights
that flicker off fences, mailboxes
on a long road in a dark night.
It's time then. It's time to drop my end
of the plastic we tore from the dry
cleaning to cover us both— we ran
at different strides and got drenched.
*By the way,* she always wants to know,
*what are you cooking for dinner tonight?*
Even if I know I say I hadn't planned.
But for her, here and now, we'll serve
roast beef, steamed broccoli, and rice,
and we'll begin the trick to change
the story into a laugh so that her legend
becomes a tale about the ordinary—
like that time, that way she asked
a cashier to do a price check at Walmart.

## She Would've Hated What I Chose

It was the dress, not the color she'd disdain.
She'd have picked a jacket, an A-line skirt
to go forward, to go Baptist into the yonder.

Although. It was blue and she favored blues:
navy for militia might, sapphire for lunches,
sky—a mother-of-the-bride nod to heaven.

I chose lapis. It was the color of the flames
in that cabin fireplace I once rented for us.
That was the time I saw her nap on the couch.

Also, I added pearls—her orbs of culture,
her stockings so she'd feel prim and warm,
her bone pumps to ease the step into bone.

She'll have to forgive me. I want her
to linger at ease in the silk folds of a long
time, in fibers that refract absence, change.

# I Try to Remember Before Her Dementia

Three days before she died
her ears curled,
the way lettuce leaves
become cups,
like the Bibb she'd fill
with chicken salad.
Off-season it was iceberg.
She'd wash, stab the greens
at the heart with a paring knife.
Her wet fingers were graceful
when she'd palm its globe,
remove the core but not nick
the layers of the head.

## The Leisure of Belief to Regulate

I placed those white, long stems
on her coffin two weeks ago.
It doesn't seem right she's dead.
As odd an idea as if she opted
for tofu instead of beef.
Whiskey, not iced tea.
A bus rather than a car.
It's just not natural she's gone—
it's like how she saw the Democrats,
the ups and downs of the Catholics,
men, but not women, with facial hair.
She had no doubts—about anything—
but she did have fears, so she fielded
all the gravity in her globe
and with her yank came a quick fall.
Now, I've seen her limits. I've known
her curled in the infancy of age.
Already I regret less and miss more
since she's not what I first thought:
a heavy foot in a '56 green Chevy.

## Washing Raspberries

It's not the death, it's the dying
that's a trap of sweet regret—
raspberries that cup rinse water.

It's not the old, it's the aging,
bodies that ripen, soft frames
that curl into hollow, hallowed

space that decays, organ by organ,
that flutters, withers into dried
hydrangeas that sere, crumble—

wiry, wispy, blue.

## The Stain Looms

like a prophet, simulacrum, holy
vision on my fifth-floor window
of the downtown office building.
A Shroud of Turin imprint
on unbroken glass near the desk
and chair—an outline that's almost
the bird that crashed into it,
in flight, the wingspan hawk-wide.
A sketch of strands in dust,
in crime-scene chalk, serene as a Zen
garden, precise as acid on an etching
so that small beads of eyeballs peer
and feathers curl like parsley,
but in the glare of tube light, stiff—
like old lady hair, the grey of lichen.
The bird crashed into the building
somewhere around Halloween,
the Day of the Dead.
For months, if I shifted my gaze
when I cradled the phone, I saw
the thing come at me, a ghost
that haunted best when light packed
it up at day's end, and I worried
it was a specter with a heavier work-
load, but it was a bird that slammed
into a day, and remained,
with a visage rain can't wash off.

## Church Bells at Midnight

The bells ring at midnight,
but the plea's not a summons.
> They're pulsed voices that call:
> *Come to locked doors. Come to a dark*
> *that links both sides of the keyhole.*

The bells strike at midnight,
and the peal's not a mourn—
> the mallet does not beat memorial.
> Not one blow of the hammer
> in the ear, in the sternum.

The bells toll at midnight,
but not glad notes for a kiss
> of a passion now shy at a wedding.
> They're brass thuds, the thump
> of the feet of Sufis in the Empty Quarter.

The bells clang at midnight,
the knell not an alarm, not
> the return of a menace who crawls
> into cribs, whispers     night is not
> absence of light but presence of dread.

The bells chime at midnight,
not a chakra, not a copper bowl
> that moans into early morning.  It's faulty
> wiring that resounds, that long moment
> when ears shoot out of deep water and ring.

## I Live Only on Streets Named for Trees

As though I want to bring in green growth, gurgle
the way dried houseplants do, make that sound
dirt makes when it gets the nurture it needs.

> Cherry Lane ran lyrical, idyllic,
> real-estate romance. Love took root
> in my first home—a rental duplex deep
> in the double names of an urban wood:
> Live Oaks, Silver Firs, Crepe Myrtle.
> But it, we, bifurcated, became loose
> debris that gathered at the grassless
> base of big trees in small yards.

As though the gnarls of my muscles and tendons
need soil in which to sink—a pull at the ends
of my hair, the fingers at my sides.

> Forest Road was an odd name for a city
> street—perhaps it was need for the rural,
> the pastoral, stained-glass light to filter
> lumber, logs to fence out change,
> to block the whine of chains.
> And that happened—front-end loaders
> slithered on treads, scooped up bricks,
> beams, the security of delusion.

As though the gray and meaty folds of my brain
want to unroll, grow tentacles of fibered
roots that creep into cracks on paved roads.

> Pine was the street of needles and cones,
> but they fell when tornado
> winds blew, when ice clutched
> and beetles gnawed, when ivy choked,
> and lightning licked like a viper,
> ran hot venom— which it all did.
> Then, the woodcutter snapped
> on crampons to climb and delimb.

As though my skin wants the layers of age—
hard bark—to crumble and compost
into mulch, lend shade to wood lice.

> Peach yields no peaches. It's a bumper
> crop of Main Street traffic, a tongue-to-ear
> breakdown of peach for pitch, tar on tar.
> But it isn't named Main, and I might not
> have moved to Main, a spot called Dead Man's
> Curve, where cars miss the twist in asphalt,
> rev up a timbred screetch of tires,
> and run down timbered and brick dwellings.

As though I can take leave, grow leaves so I
can seed, sprout, shed, then do it all again.
As though I am at home.

## Acknowledgments

*Ariadne's Thread:* "Washing Raspberries"
*Atlanta Review:* "This Is Not Another Poem About Dying"
*BorderSenses:* "I'm Not Sure If It Lessens the Import"
*Chattahoochee Review:* "Panola Mountain"
*Main Street Rag:* "Come Friday"
*Poem:* "Church Bells at Midnight"
*Poem:* "Looking for Clear Waters"
*Poeming Pigeon:* "The Family Legacy"
*Sojourner's Magazine:* "Congressman Lewis Spoke About President Obama"

*Cover artwork, "Madera Wine House" (public domain); author photo by Michael Schwarz; cover and interior book design by Diane Kistner; Georgia text and American Typewriter titling*

# About FutureCycle Press

FutureCycle Press is dedicated to publishing lasting English-language poetry books, chapbooks, and anthologies in both print-on-demand and Kindle ebook formats. Founded in 2007 by long-time independent editor/publishers and partners Diane Kistner and Robert S. King, the press incorporated as a nonprofit in 2012. A number of our editors are distinguished poets and writers in their own right, and we have been actively involved in the small press movement going back to the early seventies.

The FutureCycle Poetry Book Prize and honorarium is awarded annually for the best full-length volume of poetry we publish in a calendar year. Introduced in 2013, our Good Works projects are anthologies devoted to issues of universal significance, with all proceeds donated to a related worthy cause. Our Selected Poems series highlights contemporary poets with a substantial body of work to their credit; with this series we strive to resurrect work that has had limited distribution and is now out of print.

We are dedicated to giving all of the authors we publish the care their work deserves, making our catalog of titles the most diverse and distinguished it can be, and paying forward any earnings to fund more great books.

We've learned a few things about independent publishing over the years. We've also evolved a unique, resilient publishing model that allows us to focus mainly on vetting and preserving for posterity poetry collections of exceptional quality without becoming overwhelmed with bookkeeping and mailing, fundraising activities, or taxing editorial and production "bubbles." To find out more about what we are doing, come see us at www.futurecycle.org.

www.ingramcontent.com/pod-product-compliance
Lightning Source LLC
Chambersburg PA
CBHW070454050426
42450CB00012B/3270